CRITICAL THINKING
Reading Skills Series

• • • • • • • • • • • • • • • • •

Written by Brenda Vance Rollins, Ed. D.

GRADES 5 - 8
Reading Levels 3 - 4

Classroom Complete Press

P.O. Box 19729
San Diego, CA 92159
Tel: 1-800-663-3609 | Fax: 1-800-663-3608
Email: service@classroomcompletepress.com

www.classroomcompletepress.com

ISBN13: 978-1-55319-486-6

© 2010

Critical Thinking Skills

Critical Thinking

Skills For Critical Thinking		1	2	3	4	5	6	7	8	9	10	11	12
LEVEL 1 Remembering	Define, Duplicate, List, Memorize, Recall, Repeat, Reproduce, State	✓	✓	✓	✓	✓	✓	✓	✓	✓	✓	✓	✓
LEVEL 2 Understanding	Classify, Describe, Discuss, Explain, Identify, Locate, Recognize	✓	✓	✓	✓	✓	✓	✓	✓	✓	✓	✓	✓
LEVEL 3 Applying	Choose, Demonstrate, Dramatize, Employ, Illustrate, Interpret, Operate, Write	✓	✓	✓	✓	✓	✓	✓	✓	✓	✓	✓	✓
LEVEL 4 Analysing	Appraise, Compare, Contrast, Criticize, Differentiate, Discriminate, Distinguish, Examine	✓	✓	✓	✓	✓	✓	✓	✓	✓	✓	✓	✓
LEVEL 5 Evaluating	Argue, Defend, Judge, Select, Support, Value, Decide, Evaluate	✓		✓	✓		✓			✓	✓		✓
LEVEL 6 Creating	Assemble, Construct, Create, Design, Develop, Formulate, Write.	✓	✓	✓	✓	✓	✓	✓	✓	✓	✓	✓	✓

Based on Bloom's Taxonomy

Contents

• • • • • • • • • • • • • • • • •

TEACHER GUIDE

STUDENT HANDOUTS

EASY MARKING™ ANSWER KEY

GRAPHIC ORGANIZERS

✔ **6 BONUS** Activity Pages! **Additional worksheets for your students**   **FREE!**

- Go to our website: **www.classroomcompletepress.com/bonus**
- Enter item CC1118
- Enter pass code CC1118D for Activity Pages.

Assessment Rubric

Critical Thinking

Student's Name: _____   Assignment: _____   Level: _____

4 Consistently does <u>all or</u> almost all of the following:	• Accurately interprets evidence, statements, graphics, questions, etc. • Identifies the salient arguments (reasons and claims) pro and con. • Thoughtfully analyzes and evaluates major alternative points of view. • Draws warranted, judicious, non-fallacious conclusions. • Justifies key results and procedures, explains assumptions. • Fair-mindedly follows where evidence and reasons lead.
3 Does most or <u>many of the</u> following:	• Accurately interprets evidence, statements, graphics, questions, etc. • Identifies relevant arguments (reasons and claims) pro and con. • Offers analysis and evaluations of obvious alternative points of view. • Draws warranted, non-fallacious conclusions. • Justifies some results or procedures, explains reasons. • Fair-mindedly follows where evidence and reasons lead.
2 Does <u>most</u> or <u>many of the</u> following:	• Misinterprets evidence, statements, graphics, questions, etc. • Fails to identify strong, relevant counter-arguments. • Ignores or superficially evaluates obvious alternative points of view. • Draws unwarranted or fallacious conclusions. • Justifies few results or procedures, seldom explains reasons. • Regardless of the evidence or reasons, maintains or defends views based on self-interest or preconceptions.
1 Consistently does <u>all or</u> almost all of the following:	• Offers biased interpretations of evidence, statements, graphics, questions, information, or the points of view of others. • Fails to identify or hastily dismisses strong, relevant counter-arguments. • Ignores or superficially evaluates obvious alternative points of view. • Argues using fallacious or irrelevant reasons, and unwarranted claims. • Does not justify results or procedures, nor explain reasons. • Regardless of the evidence or reasons, maintains or defends views based on self-interest or preconceptions. • Exhibits close-mindedness or hostility to reason.

STRENGTHS:

WEAKNESSES:

NEXT STEPS:

Critical Thinking CC1118

Teacher Guide

Our resource has been created for ease of use by both TEACHERS and STUDENTS alike.

Introduction

Identifying and using critical thinking skills is a daunting task facing most elementary teachers today. Our resource was written with this very purpose in mind. Here you will find critical thinking defined as, "what happens when you judge, decide, or solve a problem." Many of the critical thinking skills such as, 1) independent thinking, 2) organization, 3) making inferences, 4) anticipating consequences, 5) recognizing valid and invalid arguments, and 6) problem solving are defined and used in thought provoking exercises throughout the book. Rather than claim to be a complete course in the process of critical thinking, this workbook is just the beginning of a critical thinking journey for students that will continue through college and into adulthood.

Our resource is designed to be user-friendly and easy to understand. Complete with vocabulary, reading passages, work sheets, graphic organizers, crossword and word search puzzles, and a comprehension quiz, *Critical Thinking* is structured using Bloom's Taxonomy of Learning to ensure educational appropriateness.

How Is Our Resource Organized?

STUDENT HANDOUTS

Reading passages and **activities** (*in the form of reproducible worksheets*) make up the majority of our resource. The reading passages present important grade-appropriate information and concepts related to the topic. Embedded in each passage are one or more questions that ensure students understand what they have read.

For each reading passage there are **BEFORE YOU READ** activities and **AFTER YOU READ** activities.

- The BEFORE YOU READ activities prepare students for reading by setting a purpose for reading. They stimulate background knowledge and experience, and guide students to make connections between what they know and what they will learn. Important concepts and vocabulary from the chapters are also presented.

- The AFTER YOU READ activities check students' comprehension of the concepts presented in the reading passage and extend their learning. Students are asked to give thoughtful consideration of the reading passage through creative and evaluative short-answer questions, research, and extension activities.

Writing Tasks are included to further develop students' thinking skills and understanding of the concepts. The **Assessment Rubric** (*page 4*) is a useful tool for evaluating students' responses to many of the activities in our resource. The **Comprehension Quiz** (*page 48*) can be used for either a follow-up review or assessment at the completion of the unit.

PICTURE CUES

This resource contains three main types of pages, each with a different purpose and use. A **Picture Cue** at the top of each page shows, at a glance, what the page is for.

Teacher Guide
- Information and tools for the teacher

Student Handout
- Reproducible worksheets and activities

Easy Marking™ Answer Key
- Answers for student activities

EASY MARKING™ ANSWER KEY

Marking students' worksheets is fast and easy with this **Answer Key**. Answers are listed in columns – just line up the column with its corresponding worksheet, as shown, and see how every question matches up with its answer!

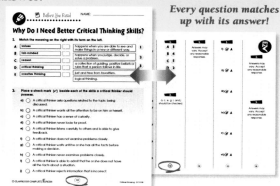

Every question matches up with its answer!

Bloom's Taxonomy* for Reading Comprehension

The activities in this resource engage and build the full range of thinking skills that are essential for students' reading comprehension. Based on the six levels of thinking in Bloom's Taxonomy, assignments are given that challenge students to not only recall what they have read, but move beyond this to understand the text through higher-order thinking. By using higher-order skills of applying, analysing, evaluating, and creating, students become active readers, drawing more meaning from the text, and applying and extending their learning in more sophisticated ways.

Our **Critical Thinking Book** is an effective tool for any Language Arts program. Whether it is used in whole or in part, or adapted to meet individual student needs, this resource provides teachers with the important questions to ask, interesting content, which promote creative and meaningful learning.

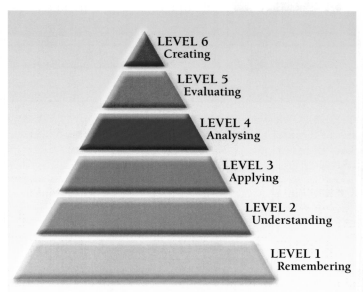

**BLOOM'S TAXONOMY:
6 LEVELS OF THINKING**

Bloom's Taxonomy is a widely used tool by educators for classifying learning objectives, and is based on the work of Benjamin Bloom.

Vocabulary

THINKING - the process of using your mind to consider something carefully.

CREATIVE THINKING - what happens when you are able to see and make things in a new or different way.

CRITICAL THINKING - what happens when you judge, decide, or solve a problem.

VALUES - a collection of guiding, positive beliefs or rules that a person follows in life.

FAIR-MINDED - just and free from favoritism.

REASON - logical thinking.

INDEPENDENT THINKING - feeling free to make choices.

ORGANIZED - orderly and effective.

INFERENCE - a conclusion you come to in your mind based on something else that you believe to be true.

FACTS - clearly stated information that can be proven.

OPINIONS - beliefs that are based on feelings that cannot be proven.

ANTICIPATE - expect.

CONSEQUENCES - the effects or results of a decision or an action.

FOUR TYPES OF CRITICAL QUESTIONS - getting the facts, evaluating the facts, drawing a conclusion using logic, and evaluating the conclusion.

PROBLEMS - states of difficulty that need to be settled or questions that need to be answered.

FIVE TYPES OF CRITICAL PROBLEM SOLVING - define the problem and set a goal for change, brainstorm possible solutions or answers, evaluate all the possible solutions, choose a solution and make a plan of action, and evaluation and modification.

MODIFICATIONS - changes.

ATTRIBUTES - characteristics.

MANIPULATED - controlled.

Before You Read

What are Critical Thinking Skills?

1. (Circle) the word True if the statement is true. (Circle) the word False if it's false.

a) Everybody uses their brains in the same way.

    True   **False**

b) Learning about thinking is important.

    True   **False**

c) A person cannot become a better thinker by practicing critical thinking skills.

    True   **False**

d) There are several kinds of thinking.

    True   **False**

2. On your classroom computer, go to http://www.youtube.com/view_play_list?p=AE062FAC5DAAF012. Click "Play all videos" and watch the following videos closely. After you've finished watching the videos, answer the following questions.

Place a check mark (✔) beside the correct answer to each question.

i) Why is Fair-minded Fran good at thinking?

○ **A** **She was born with a brilliant brain.**

○ **B** **She practices thinking every day.**

○ **C** **She only reads books about how to think.**

ii) When Fran is confused she _____.

○ **A** **asks questions.**

○ **B** **cries.**

○ **C** **asks her mom for help every time.**

iii) Selfish Sam _____

○ **A** **believes whatever he wants to believe.**

○ **B** **believes what he can prove.**

○ **C** **believes nothing.**

iv) Naïve Nancy _____.

○ **A** **never believes anyone.**

○ **B** **believes most of what she sees and hears.**

○ **C** **only believes what she wants to.**

What are Critical Thinking Skills?

Thinking is defined as "the process of using your mind to carefully consider something." Thinking is something you do every minute that you are awake. Some people even believe that dreaming is another way that your mind thinks about things.

There are many types of thinking. Two of the most important are creative thinking and critical thinking. **Creative thinking** is what happens when you are able to see and make things in a new or different way. Any time you write a poem or draw a picture you are using creative thinking.

Critical thinking happens when you judge, decide, or solve a problem. Whenever you must figure out what to believe or what to do, you are using critical thinking skills. One good way to understand critical thinking is to picture in your mind what a judge does at a trial. Judges are fair, open-minded, and respectful. They listen to both sides of an argument and look carefully at all of the evidence before they reach a decision or make a judgment. They also ask questions of the people involved in the trial and then use their critical thinking skills to come up with the best verdict (or decision) possible. You can be a critical thinker just like the judges that were described.

Think about your classmates. Some of them decide to think just like their friends. Others may argue about everything without giving good reasons why something shouldn't be done. Some may just stand back and do or say nothing. The critical thinkers in the crowd will think about the topic, ask questions, do some research if needed, and then make a fair decision based on facts.

There are many skills involved in critical thinking. The ones we will study in this workbook are: (1) independent thinking, (2) organization, (3) making inferences, (4) anticipating consequences, (5) recognizing valid and invalid arguments, and (6) problem solving.

You can learn to be a critical thinker. The goal of our resource is to teach you to use the skills listed above in order to make the best decisions possible in school and in your life.

The Reading Watch Dog says,
"Critical thinking is the process of reasonably deciding what to believe or do."

What are Critical Thinking Skills?

1. **Fill in each blank with the correct term.**

a) Two important types of thinking are _____ thinking and _____ thinking.

b) _____ is defined as "the process of using your mind to consider something carefully."

c) _____ thinking is what happens when you are able to see and make things in a new or different way.

d) _____ thinking happens when you judge, decide, or solve a problem.

2. **In the chart below, decide whether or not each activity requires you to use critical thinking skills, then put a check in the correct box.**

Everyday Life Activities	Involves Critical Thinking	Does NOT Involve Critical Thinking
a) Buying a new bike		
b) Choosing the best lawnmower for the family		
c) Brushing your teeth		
d) Moving to a new house		
e) Talking on the phone with your best friend		
f) Spending your $10 allowance		
g) Jogging		
h) Planning a vacation for the family		

Why Do I Need Better Critical Thinking Skills?

1.   Match the meaning on the right with its term on the left.

A values	**1** happens when you are able to see and make things in a new or different way.
B fair-minded	**2** happens when you judge, decide, or solve a problem.
C reason	**3** a collection of guiding, positive beliefs or rules that a person follows in life.
D critical thinking	**4** just and free from favoritism.
E creative thinking	**5** logical thinking.

2.   Place a check mark (✔) beside each of the skills a critical thinker should possess.

a) ◯ A critical thinker asks questions related to the topic being discussed.

b) ◯ A critical thinker wants all the attention to be on him or herself.

c) ◯ A critical thinker has a sense of curiosity.

d) ◯ A critical thinker never looks for proof.

e) ◯ A critical thinker listens carefully to others and is able to give feedback.

f) ◯ A critical thinker does not examine problems closely.

g) ◯ A critical thinker waits until he or she has all the facts before making a decision.

h) ◯ A critical thinker never examines problems closely.

i) ◯ A critical thinker is able to admit that he or she does not have all the facts about a situation.

j) ◯ A critical thinker rejects information that is incorrect.

Why Do I Need Better Critical Thinking Skills?

There are many reasons why students should learn to use critical thinking skills. These reasons are called a set of values for critical thinkers. **Values** are a collection of guiding, positive beliefs or rules that a person follows in life.

The first reason to be a critical thinker **is to become able to think for yourself, instead of accepting what others want you to believe without question**. In the before you read section from the first chapter, Naïve Nancy didn't think for herself. She even stated that it's easier to let someone else think for her. Naïve Nancy is definitely not a critical thinker!

The next reason to learn critical thinking skills is because **critical thinkers welcome the chance to explore new ideas and points of view**. In the before you read section from the first chapter, Fair-minded Fran was happy to learn new things and to go to new places. Having an attitude like this makes life an exciting adventure.

Another good reason to be a critical thinker is that **critical thinkers use reason to find the answers to questions, judge ideas, and solve conflicts**. In this case, reason is logical thinking. Critical thinkers don't just make up answers to questions or decide they don't like a person because of the clothes they wear or the way their voice sounds. They are fair and just to everyone.

The Reading Watch Dog says,

"Critical thinkers:
- *Distinguish between fact and opinion*
- *Ask questions*
- *Make detailed observations*
- *Uncover assumptions and define their terms*
- *Make assertions based on sound logic and solid evidence"*

An excellent reason to develop critical thinking skills is **to learn to include the opinions of many different people in your discussions**. Good teachers try to follow this guideline in their classrooms. Think back to a time when your class was having a good discussion about an interesting subject. How would you have felt if your teacher had not let you express your own ideas and thoughts?

Judging ideas based on how good they are and not on the person who thought of them is another reason to become a good critical thinker. And finally, the last reason for studying critical thinking is because **critical thinkers achieve the best possible solution to problems, instead of wanting to win arguments just for the sake of winning them.**

All of these reasons show us that being a critical thinker is a very valuable tool to have. Now let's see what we need to do in order to gain all these skills.

Why Do I Need Better Critical Thinking Skills?

1. **Look carefully at the picture. How do you think this picture is related to the need for better critical thinking skills?**

    After looking at the picture, answer the following questions:

a) **What do you see in the picture?**

    _____

    _____

    _____

    _____

b) **What do you think the picture represents?**

    _____

    _____

    _____

    _____

c) **How does the picture relate to the need for better critical thinking skills?**

    _____

    _____

    _____

    _____

Keys to Independent Thinking

1. Are you an independent thinker? Take this quiz and find out! Place a check mark
(✔) beside the correct answer to each question.

i) If you found a dollar on the floor of the classroom you would:

○ **A** **quietly give the money to your teacher because someone might need it for lunch.**

○ **B** **keep the money and spend it at the store on the way home from school.**

○ **C** **give the money to your teacher and make sure that everyone knows that you did this good deed.**

ii) When you are learning a new skill you try and fail the first few times you try. Then you:

○ **A** **smile and keep on trying.**

○ **B** **wait and practice at home where no one can see you.**

○ **C** **lose interest and try something else that is easier.**

iii) When something goes wrong in your life you:

○ **A** **find a solution.**

○ **B** **find someone to blame.**

○ **C** **blame someone else and then try to find a solution.**

iv) You tell things that are not true:

○ **A** **almost never.**

○ **B** **all the time.**

○ **C** **about as much as the next kid.**

v) When it comes to belonging to a group you:

○ **A** **don't worry if you're not in the "popular" group.**

○ **B** **worry just a little bit about being in the popular group.**

○ **C** **worry tremendously if you're not in the "in crowd."**

vi) You are honest with yourself:

○ **A** **almost all the time.**

○ **B** **sometimes.**

○ **C** **never.**

> **If you marked "A" 5 or 6 times, you are a very independent thinker. If you marked "A" 3 or 4 times, you are almost an independent thinker. If you marked "A" 2 or fewer times, you need to work on your independent thinking skills.**

Keys to Independent Thinking

A critical thinker is an independent thinker. Critical thinkers make decisions for themselves, not because someone else tells them what to think. They know that independent thinking is a skill that can be learned by practicing making decisions.

The **key to thinking independently is the ability to make choices**. If you learn to think critically and independently you're far less likely to make poor choices that are harmful to yourself or to others. <u>You should practice making decisions</u>. The more decisions you make, the better decision-maker you'll become.

Independent thinkers share their ideas and opinions with others. By sharing ideas you will open a line of communication and encourage your friends to share their ideas and opinions with you. Being able to communicate is a skill that all critical thinkers must have.

Independent thinkers are good listeners. Listening is a vital part of communication. You might talk for hours, but until someone listens to what you are saying there is no communication. Also, one of the best ways to learn is to listen.

Independent thinkers are honest and fair-minded. After sharing their own ideas and opinions, independent thinkers gladly listen with an open mind to their friends' ideas and opinions. If you want to become an independent thinker you must remember to be honest about what you tell others. There is no place for lying in the mind of a good independent thinker.

The Reading Watch Dog says,

"Independent thinking means making sense of the world based on your own observations and experiences rather than just depending on the word of others. It means trusting your own ability to make judgments, even if they go against what others say. It means acting according to these judgments, even if you sometimes make mistakes. An independent thinker knows it's better to make mistakes than to accept someone else's opinions about everything in life."

NAME: _____

Keys to Independent Thinking

1. **Reread the article on page 14 about "Keys to Independent Thinking" and then list at least four qualities that most independent thinkers have.**

All independent thinkers:

a) _____

b) _____

c) _____

d) _____

2. On your classroom or home computer, go to http://www.biography.com/bio4kids/index.jsp. Choose one person from the list below. Click on "Meet the People" and find and read that person's biography. Then list as many examples of that person's critical or independent thinking as you can find.

> **Albert Einstein   Amelia Earhart   Barack Obama   Benjamin Franklin   J.K. Rowling**
> **Frida Kahlo   Davy Crockett   Christa McAuliffe   Babe Ruth   Paul Revere**

Person's Name: _____

Examples of his or her independent thinking: *(Use complete sentences)*

_____

_____

_____

_____

_____

_____

_____

_____

NAME: _____

Keys to Organization

1. **Place a check mark (✔) next to each sentence that describes an organized critical thinker.**

a) ◯ At the beginning of each school year, Maria writes a list of the things she wants to achieve during the year. She checks this list often.

b) ◯ In the morning, Raymond sleeps until it is almost time for the school bus. Then he has to run around his room to find his clothes, shoes, and books.

c) ◯ Billy decides what he's going to wear to school and lays it out on his dresser the night before.

d) ◯ Chrissy's room is filled with crumpled papers and old homework assignments. She never knows where anything is.

e) ◯ Keith keeps a list of the things he has to do for school in his notebook.

f) ◯ Kevin watches TV until late at night on school nights. Then he oversleeps and has to rush to get to school on time.

g) ◯ Mario tries to eat three balanced meals each day. He wants to keep his body strong and healthy.

h) ◯ Joe leaves his student planner at home most of the time and never seems to know when an assignment is due.

i) ◯ Parker plays some type of sport every school night. He is always rushing to finish his homework and never spends time with his parents.

j) ◯ Janice has a special place in her home to do her homework each night.

2. **In the box opposite, design a poster that has at least one good hint for staying organized in it.**

Keys to Organization

A critical thinker is an organized or "orderly and effective" thinker. Many students think in a very unorganized or confusing way. They might be listening to the teacher one second and wondering about what's on TV the next. When unorganized thinkers sit down to do their homework, they have to hunt for the assignment sheet, find their pencils and paper, and then ask their parents what the directions mean. In other words, they don't get much thinking done! A good critical thinker is just the opposite.

A student who is organized has a system or routine in place that includes the following:

- A way to make sure he or she has all the tools he or she needs for homework and schoolwork.
- Places to keep supplies both at home and at school.
- A way to transport his or her books and supplies between home and school when necessary.
- A way to make sure parents receive papers and forms for signing.
- A way to return those papers and forms to school.
- A way to stay on top of test dates and due dates.

Critical thinkers have a special place to study and work at home. It doesn't have to be a whole room, a desk or table will do. **The place needs to have a good light source and a quiet atmosphere.** You should be ready to think when you go to your special study area.

Critical thinkers need a system to keep track of important papers. Many students use a three ring binder with special folders in it. In this binder you can keep your homework sheets, notes that need to be signed, and other important material that you need to save.

Critical thinkers need to have a calendar or datebook for assignments and due dates. A calendar will help you keep track of everything that needs to be returned to your teacher.

Critical thinkers make sure that they understand their short-term and long-term assignments. You should listen carefully to your teacher and then ask questions if you don't understand any part of the assignment. Being organized leaves you the time to get down to your real work — THINKING!

The Reading Watch Dog says,

"Out of clutter, find Simplicity. From discord, find Harmony. In the middle of difficulty lies opportunity."
— Albert Einstein, Scientist.

Keys to Organization

1. Use the space provided below to write at least three paragraphs about "How to be an Organized Student." You may use your dictionary if you need to.

_____

_____

_____

_____

_____

_____

_____

_____

_____

_____

_____

_____

_____

_____

_____

_____

_____

_____

_____

_____

_____

_____

_____

Keys to Inferences

1. (Circle) the word True if the statement is true. (Circle) the word False if it's false.

a) An inference is a conclusion you come to in your mind based on something else that you believe to be true.

    True   **False**

b) The things that you believe to be <u>not true</u> are called your assumptions.

    True   **False**

c) Facts are clearly stated information that can be proven.

    True   **False**

d) Beliefs that are only based on feelings are called hunches.

    True   **False**

e) A sentence using the words, "probably" and "I think" is most likely a fact.

    True   **False**

2. **Put an "F" in front of each FACT and put an "O" in front of each OPINION.**

a) ☐   My dad drives a red convertible.

b) ☐   It's the most beautiful car in our neighborhood.

c) ☐   All the kids believe that I am the luckiest person in the world!

d) ☐   The car is three years old.

e) ☐   It cost $21,000.

Keys to Inferences

Making inferences is an important part of the critical thinking process. **An inference is a conclusion you come to in your mind based on something else that you believe to be true.** The things that you believe to be true are called your **assumptions**. For example, if I walk toward you smiling and with my right hand held out, you will probably infer that I am friendly and want to shake hands with you. You made that inference based on the fact that you have had experiences like this one in the past. You made the inference that I wanted to be friendly because others who acted the same way were friendly to you.

You have learned that **facts are clearly stated information that can be proven**. Critical thinkers should base their assumptions on facts, not feelings. **Beliefs that are based on feelings are called opinions.** Opinions cannot be proven. If you said that the earth is round, the statement would be a fact. It can be proven. Astronauts have taken pictures from space that show that the earth is round. However, if you say that the picture of the earth from space is the most beautiful photograph ever taken, the statement is an opinion. It is based on your feelings about the photograph.

There are many words that will give you a hint about a statement being a fact or an opinion. They are:

Words that Signal Opinions

Does the author use words that interpret or label, such as:

pretty, ugly, safe, dangerous, evil, attractive, well-dressed, good, and so on?

Are there words that clue you to statements of opinion, such as:

probably, perhaps, usually, often, sometimes, on occasion, I believe, I think, in my opinion, I feel, I suggest?

The Reading Watch Dog says,
"A fact is based on direct evidence, actual experience, or observation."

Keys to Inferences

1. **Read each sentence and choose the most logical inference. In the space provided, explain why that inference makes sense.**

i) Bits of paper danced across the parking lot.

○ **A** **It is a hot day.**
○ **B** **It is a windy day.**
○ **C** **It is a cold evening.**
○ **D** **It is snowing.**

> Why do you think so?

ii) Joe put on his suit and tie.

○ **A** **Joe is on his way to church.**
○ **B** **Joe looks good in blue.**
○ **C** **Joe is going to dig in the garden.**
○ **D** **Joe needs to dress nicely.**

> Why do you think so?

iii) All the girls were asleep.

○ **A** **The room must be pretty dark.**
○ **B** **It may be noon.**
○ **C** **It must be late at night.**
○ **D** **The room must be hot.**

> Why do you think so?

iv) The kitten's fur was fluffy and smelled good.

○ **A** **The kitten just stepped in mud.**
○ **B** **The kitten just ran into a skunk.**
○ **C** **The kitten just woke up from a nap.**
○ **D** **The kitten just had a bath.**

> Why do you think so?

v) The children just left for school.

○ **A** **It's midnight.**
○ **B** **It's morning.**
○ **C** **It's bedtime.**
○ **D** **It's late afternoon.**

> Why do you think so?

Keys to Anticipating Consequences

1. **Circle** the answer that correctly completes each statement.

a) _____ are the effects or results of a decision or an action.

    i) Surprises   **ii) Consequences**   **iii) Conditions**

b) _____ means "expect or look forward to."

    i) Suppose   **ii) Worry**   **iii) Anticipate**

c) Another way of saying "anticipate consequences" is _____.

    i)   **"Look before you leap!"**

    ii) **"Don't count your chickens before they hatch!"**

    iii) **"Two heads are better than one."**

d) _____ is *not* a characteristic of a good critical thinker.

    i)   **Planning ahead**

    ii) **Jumping to conclusions**

    iii) **Being honest with himself**

e) Critical thinking is a(n) _____ process.

    i) active   **ii) slow**   **iii) very difficult**

2. Complete the following graphic organizer about "Anticipating Consequences."

Anticipating Consequences	
Action or Plan	**Things that Could Happen**
Changing the rules to a game while you and your friends are playing it.	
Driving without a driver's license.	

Keys to Anticipating Consequences

A critical thinker plans ahead and anticipates or expects consequences. Consequences are the effects or results of a decision or an action. Suppose that you are in the middle of a large park on a very hot day. Suddenly, you look to your left and see a shimmering blue swimming pool. Your first thought would be to run to it and jump in, but should you? Probably not before you stop and think about the consequences. You might ask yourself these kinds of questions: "Is there a locked fence all the way around the pool?"; "Has the water just been treated with chemicals?"; "Is there a 'KEEP OUT' sign on the gate?"; "Is the water deep enough to dive in?"; or "Is there a policeman guarding the pool?"

Another way of saying "anticipate consequences" is "look before you leap!" Stop and think about what might happen if you make the decision you'd planned on or if you change the rules of a game or project. Will there be problems that you must solve because you didn't anticipate the consequences? Good critical thinking means being careful, taking enough time to be thoughtful, and not jumping to conclusions.

Failing to anticipate the consequences of your decisions can lead to bad results for you as the decision maker and for other people as well. What if your ball rolled off the sidewalk, between two parked cars and onto the street? Would you run from between the cars to rescue your ball? Hopefully, you would not! If you are a critical thinker you will stop and think about the consequences of running into the street to get a ball. You might just save your own or someone else's life.

Critical thinking is an active process. Stopping to anticipate the consequences of decisions or actions is something that most critical thinkers do throughout the day. Critical thinkers are honest with themselves. After you've thought about all the possible results or effects of your decision, you honestly make a decision about whether to go ahead. Finally, critical thinkers ask questions. By asking questions, it becomes easier to gather all the facts you need to make good decisions. A critical thinker is an informed thinker.

The Reading Watch Dog says,

"The key to wisdom is the anticipation of consequences."

Keys to Anticipating Consequences

LOST AT SEA *You have rented a big boat with three friends. You want to travel in the Atlantic Ocean from Virginia Beach, VA down to the Caribbean island of Jamaica. You have hired an experienced captain. Unfortunately, in the Atlantic a huge storm breaks out and the captain is knocked unconscious. Much of the boat is destroyed and is slowly sinking. Your location is unclear because your radio equipment has been damaged in the storm. Your best guess is that you are hundreds of miles from the nearest land. You and your friends have managed to save 15 items from the storm. Also, you have saved a four man rubber life raft and a box of matches. Your job is to rank the 15 items in terms of their importance for you, as you wait to be rescued. Place the number 1 by the most important item, the number 2 by the second most important, and so on through to number 15 for the least important.*

MY RANKING	SALVAGED ITEMS	+ or – Coast Guard Score
	A sextant (navigational instrument)	
	A mirror	
	Some mosquito netting	
	A 25 liter container of water	
	army rations (freeze-dried food)	
	Maps of the Pacific Ocean	
	A floating seat cushion	
	A 10 liter can of gasoline mixture	
	A small radio	
	Black plastic sheeting	
	A can of shark repellent	
	One bottle of rum (alcoholic drink)	
	15 ft nylon rope	
	2 boxes of chocolate bars	
	A fishing kit	
TOTAL		**TOTAL**

Your teacher will compare your score with the Coast Guard's list of most important items. The lower your score is the better! ___

0 - 25 Excellent. You demonstrated great survival skills. Rescued!
26 - 32 Good. Above average results. Good survival skills. Rescued!
33 - 45 Average. Seasick, hungry and tired. Rescued!
46 - 55 Fair. Dehydrated and barely alive. It was tough, but rescued!
56 - 70 Poor. Rescued, but only just in time!
71 - 112 Very poor. Oh dear, your empty raft is washed up on a beach, weeks after the search was called off.

Keys to Asking Questions (Part One)

1. **Put an "F" in front of each FACT and put an "O" in front of each OPINION.**

a) ☐ The President's tax package will solve all the government's financial problems.

b) ☐ Seatbelts can help prevent injuries and deaths.

c) ☐ The jury found the man was guilty based on the evidence that was presented.

d) ☐ The Governor's mansion is the fanciest house in the state.

e) ☐ Abraham Lincoln was the most intelligent president we have ever had.

f) ☐ Paris is the most interesting city in Europe.

g) ☐ Every statement printed in a newspaper is a fact.

h) ☐ Fast-food restaurants should not give away toys to children.

i) ☐ Most birds migrate in the winter.

j) ☐ Apple's iPhone is the best cell phone ever made.

2. **Circle the word True if the statement is true. Circle the word False if it's false.**

a) A big part of critical thinking is asking the right questions.

   True   **False**

b) Critical thinkers should always let their emotions mix with their decisions.

   True   **False**

c) Critical thinking happens when you say the first thing that comes to your mind.

   True   **False**

d) A good critical thinker can always change the facts to suit his or her wishes.

   True   **False**

e) There are four types of critical thinking questions.

   True   **False**

Keys to Asking Questions (Part One)

A good critical thinker asks many questions. Questions are one of the driving forces of critical thinking. Learning to ask the right kinds of questions is one of the most important skills a critical thinker can have. **Clear and exact questions lead to clear and exact answers.**

You may be thinking that you have always asked questions, so what's the big deal? The "big deal" is that you may not have received as much information as you needed from the questions you asked. Remember that critical thinking happens when you judge, decide, or solve a problem. Questions are the tools you use to do these things.

There are four types of critical thinking questions. They are: (1) Getting the Facts, (2) Evaluating the Facts, (3) Drawing a Conclusion using Logic, and (4) Evaluating a Conclusion.

The first type of critical thinking question is **Getting the Facts**. Tools for Getting the Facts include questions like "Who?", "What?", "Where?", "When?", and "How?" You should remember that facts are clearly stated information that can be proven. Make sure that you don't let your emotions influence the facts that you gather. You may not like all the facts that you learn from the answers you get, but you must be honest in order to be a good critical thinker.

The second type of critical thinking questions is **Evaluating the Facts**. Evaluation is "the process of examining pieces of information and rating them based on a given set of rules or beliefs. This means that a critical thinker takes the answers he or she receives and then decides if each one is truly a fact, if it is related to the problem being solved, and if it can be used to solve the problem.

We will discuss the remaining two types of critical thinking questions in the next lesson.

The Reading Watch Dog says,
"The key to a clear understanding is listening and asking the right questions."

Keys to Asking Questions (Part One)

1. Use the graphic organizer below to write five "Getting the Facts" questions about the following article.

Farmers Use Falcons to Protect Berries

Rather than using chemicals or noise to keep birds from eating their ripe berries, some farmers are trying a new way to scare off hungry birds — bigger birds. Farmers in some parts of the U.S. have hired people who own falcons, which are large birds of prey, to guard their berries. Small birds called starlings love berries. They can destroy hundreds of thousands of dollars in berries each year. But starlings are afraid of falcons, so they fly off when they see one nearby. Farmers use falcons that are trained not to kill the starlings and to fly back to their owners.

Keeping an eye on the falcons is hard work. One man and his eight trained falcons worked last summer at Rose's Berry Farm in Glastonbury, Connecticut. They worked 11 hours a day, seven days a week, to chase starlings from the farm.

In the past, the Roses tried chemicals and even small cannons to scare away the birds. But the chemical is no longer sold and the neighbors did not like the noise from the cannons. The Roses thought about covering their 40 acres of blueberries with nets to protect them, but the netting would have been very expensive.

http://www.education-world.com/a_lesson/newsforyou/pdfs/newsforyou101.pdf

---

Getting the Facts by Asking Questions
Who?
What?
Where?
When?
Why?
How?

2. Write three facts that you read in the news article above and write what you could do to prove each one. (Use complete sentences.)

1) _____

2) _____

3) _____

Keys to Asking Questions (Part Two)

1.   Match the meaning on the right with its term on the left.

A	**conclusion**			a method that investigates arguments.	**1**
B	**relevance**			how facts are related to a question.	**2**
C	**significance**			judge the facts and to decide which ones are important.	**3**
D	**evaluate**			a statement that sums up all of the information collected in order to make a point or a decision.	**4**
E	**logic**			unacceptable.	**5**
F	**invalid**			how important the facts are to the question.	**6**

2.   Number the steps in the Critical Questioning Process from 1 to 4 in the correct order.

a) ☐   "Drawing a Conclusion Using Logic."

b) ☐   "Getting the Facts."

c) ☐   "Evaluating a Conclusion."

d) ☐   "Evaluating the Facts."

Keys to Asking Questions (Part Two)

You learned in the last chapter that there are four keys to asking critical questions. They are: (1) Getting the Facts, (2) Evaluating the Facts, (3) Drawing a Conclusion using Logic, and (4) Evaluating a Conclusion. "Getting the Facts" questions are those asking "the 5 Ws + H" — who, what, where, when, why, and how. 5 Ws + H questions help to make the facts more clear. "Evaluating the Facts" questions help you decide which facts you should use to draw a conclusion. Evaluating the Facts questions explore the relevance (how the facts are related to the question) and the significance (how important the facts are to the question) of the facts.

The next critical thinking question is the "Drawing a Conclusion using Logic" type. A conclusion is a statement that sums up all of the information you have collected in order to make a point or a decision. Think of a police officer investigating a traffic accident. He or she first asks "Getting the facts" questions, such as, "Was the light green when you came to it?" or "Did you stop at the stop sign?" When all the facts have been gathered, the officer will then decide which ones are important by asking the "Evaluating the Facts" questions, such as, "Is this fact related to the question?"

Next, it's the officer's job to evaluate or **judge the facts and to decide which ones are important by asking "Drawing a Conclusion using Logic" questions**. For example, one driver might not like people in red cars. This driver might want to say that it was not the missing stop sign that caused the accident, but that it was the man in the red car that caused it because "men in red cars always cause accidents." Is this true, or is the driver making a mistake in logic? "Drawing a Conclusion" questions use **logic (a method that investigates arguments)** to help critical thinkers avoid making the wrong decision by deciding how true the driver's explanation is. Do men in red cars always cause accidents? If not, the driver has reached an invalid (unacceptable) conclusion.

The fourth kind of critical question is "Evaluating the Conclusion." An excellent example of this type is, "Let me understand what you are saying. Are you saying (that all red cars cause accidents)?" Repeating the conclusion the person has reached often helps both parties decide if it is acceptable or unacceptable.

The Reading Watch Dog says,

"Check out these examples of each of the four critical questioning tools:"

Types of Critical Question	Examples
Getting the Facts Questions	"Who?" "What?" "Where?" "When?" "Why?" and "How?"
Evaluating the Facts Questions	"Is this fact relevant or significant?" "Is this fact substantial, crucial, and applicable?" and "Does it support the conclusion?"
Drawing a Conclusion Using Logic Questions	"Is this valid and consistent with other information?" and "Are there any logical flaws in this conclusion?"
Evaluating a Conclusion Questions	"Is this fair and reasonable?" and "Does my conclusion have the necessary depth and breadth?"

NAME: _____

Keys to Asking Questions (Part Two)

1. **Pretend that you are the attorney who is trying to prove that Alexander Wolf is guilty of murdering two of the three little pigs. Read his testimony below. Then make up at least one of each of the four kinds of critical thinking questions about it. Write your questions in the space provided below.**

Here is Wolf's testimony:

"Everybody thinks they know the story of the Three Little Pigs. But I'll let you in on a little secret. Nobody knows the real story, because nobody has ever heard my side of the story. The real story is about a sneeze and a cup of sugar.

THIS IS THE REAL STORY.

A few weeks ago, I was making a birthday cake for my dear old granny. I had a terrible sneezing cold. I ran out of sugar. So I walked down the street to ask my neighbor for a cup of sugar. Now this neighbor was a pig. And he wasn't too bright either. He had built his whole house out of straw. Can you believe it? So of course the minute I knocked on the door, it fell right in. I didn't want to just walk into someone else's house. So I called, "Little Pig, Little Pig, are you in?" No answer. I was just about to go home without the cup of sugar for my dear old granny's birthday cake.

That's when my nose started to itch. I felt a sneeze coming on. Well I huffed. And I snuffed. And I sneezed a great sneeze.

And you know what? That straw house fell down. And right in the middle of the pile of straw was the First Little Pig — dead as a doornail. He had been home the whole time. It seemed like a shame to leave a perfectly good ham dinner lying there in the straw. So I ate it up. I was feeling a little better. But I still didn't have my cup of sugar. So I went to the next neighbor's house. This neighbor was the First Little Pig's brother. He was a little smarter, but not much. He had built his house of sticks. I rang the bell on the stick house. Nobody answered. I called, "Mr. Pig, Mr. Pig, are you in?" He yelled back. "Go away wolf. You can't come in. I'm shaving the hairs on my chinny-chin-chin."

I had just grabbed the doorknob when I felt another sneeze coming on. I huffed. And I snuffed. And I tried to cover my mouth, but I sneezed a great sneeze.

And you are not going to believe this, but the pig's house fell down just like his brother's. When the dust cleared, there was the Second Little Pig — dead as a doornail. Wolf's honor. Now you know food will spoil if you just leave it out in the open. So I did the only thing there was to do. I had dinner again. Think of it as a second helping. I was getting awfully full. But my cold was feeling a little better. And I still didn't have that cup of sugar for my dear old granny's birthday cake.

I went to the next house. This pig was the First and Second Little Pig's brother. He must have been the brains of the family. He had built his house of bricks. I knocked on the brick house. No answer. I called, "Mr. Pig, Mr. Pig, are you in?" And do you know what that rude little porker answered? "Get out of here, Wolf. Don't bother me again."

Talk about impolite! He probably had a whole sack full of sugar. And he wouldn't give me even one little cup for my dear sweet old granny's birthday cake. What a pig!

I was just about to go home and maybe make a nice birthday card instead of a cake, when I felt my cold coming on. I huffed And I snuffed. And I sneezed once again.

Then the Third Little Pig yelled, "And your old granny can sit on a pin!" Now I'm usually a pretty calm fellow. But when somebody talks about my granny like that, I go a little crazy. When the police drove up, of course I was trying to break down this Pig's door. And the whole time I was huffing and puffing and sneezing and making a real scene. The rest as they say is history.

---

a) Getting the Facts question (5 Ws + H): _____

b) Evaluating the Facts question (Are the facts related to the question?): _____

_____

c) Drawing a Conclusion Using Logic question (Is the answer logical? Does it make sense?):

_____

d) Evaluating Conclusions question: _____

Keys to Problem Solving (Part One)

1. **Answer each question with a complete sentence.**

a) What do you think the phrase, "problem solving" means?

_____

_____

b) Describe at least two kinds of problems that a student like you might need to solve.

_____

_____

c) A man is looking at a photograph of someone. His friend asks who it is. The man replies, "Brothers and sisters, I have none. But that man's father is my father's son." Who was in the photograph?

_____

d) Before Mt. Everest was discovered, what was the highest mountain in the world?

_____

e) Jimmy's mother had 4 children. She named the first Monday. She named the second Tuesday. The third was named Wednesday. What is the name of the fourth child?

_____

2. Circle the word True if the statement is true. Circle the word False if it's false.

a) Everyone has problems that need to be solved.

True   **False**

b) The best solution to a problem is to ask your mother or father what to do about it.

True   **False**

c) When there is a problem to be solved, using the first answer you think of is always the best solution.

True   **False**

d) Brainstorming means sitting down by yourself or with friends and coming up with as many possible solutions to the problem as you can.

True   **False**

NAME: _____

Keys to Problem Solving (Part One)

Everyday life is filled with problems. You may have a disagreement with one of your friends. Or you may have a word problem to solve in math or science. Everyone has problems and everyone needs to learn problem-solving skills. **Problems are defined as, "states of difficulty that need to be settled or questions that need to be answered." Knowing how to solve problems is a very important critical thinking skill.**

Problem solving is a process with five steps. To be a better critical thinker you should learn and use this process anytime you have a problem. **The first step in critical problem solving is: Define the problem and set a goal for change.** You could have difficulty with a process or a problem and still be unsure about what is wrong. When this happens, you must stop and look at the situation. Ask questions like, "What is needed here?", "What is not working?", or "Why did this happen?", and then "How should this be different?"

The second step in critical problem solving is, "Brainstorm possible solutions or answers." Brainstorming means sitting down by yourself or with friends and coming up with as many possible solutions to the problem as you can. During the brainstorming session, no answer is too silly or simple to list.

The third step in critical problem solving is, "Evaluate all the possible solutions." During this evaluation you should decide whether or not a given solution is possible. Other things to consider are what you will need to make a solution work and whether or not the solution is something that you can do by yourself.

We will discuss the last two steps in the problem solving process in the next chapter.

The Reading Watch Dog says,
"To live is to have problems, and to solve problems is to grow intellectually."

Keys to Problem Solving (Part One)

1. **Explain what the following steps in critical problem solving mean. (Use complete sentences.)**

    a) Define the problem and set a goal for change.

    _____

    _____

    b) Brainstorm possible solutions or answers.

    _____

    _____

    c) Evaluate all the possible solutions.

    _____

    _____

2. **In complete sentences, explain how you would solve each of the following problems. Remember, your goal is to be as independent as possible, but don't be afraid to ask for help.**

    a) There are leaves all over your front yard. Dad left $20 and said that you should solve the problem. What will you do?

    _____

    _____

    b) You are in the house alone and you have just cut your finger. The blood is dripping onto the floor. What will you do to solve the problem?

    _____

    _____

    c) You are in your homeroom and you realize that you have ripped the seat out of your pants. What will you do to solve this problem?

    _____

    _____

Keys to Problem Solving (Part Two)

1. **Answer each question in complete sentences.**

a) What does the word, "problem" mean?

_____

_____

b) Describe the first three steps in the critical problem solving process.

_____

_____

2. **Use your problem solving skills to find the right answer in each of the following situations.**

a) Problem:

Luis, Maria, and Sandy, were all over at Keith's house when a package was delivered. Each child guessed what was in the box, but only one of them was right. Using their guesses as clues, can you figure out what was in the box?

Maria said, "It's a laptop computer." Sandy said, "I'll bet it's a pizza." Luis said, "I think a picture or a laptop computer is in the box." "It's a picture, for sure," said Keith.

What's in the Mystery Box? _____

b) Problem:

Someone's dog goes around the neighborhood every night getting into people's garbage pails and making a mess. Some of the neighborhood kids say they know what the guilty dog looks like, but the culprit strikes at night, so it's hard to see. Each of the four witnesses has one and only one detail right, and each detail is described correctly by only one witness.

Don says the dog is white, fluffy, wears a red collar, and has a long tail. Kathy says the dog is black, has short hair, wears a red collar, and has a long tail. Meno says the dog is brown, has long, silky hair, wears a blue collar, and has a long tail. Emily says the dog is spotted, fluffy, wears a red collar, and has a short tail.

What does the guilty dog look like? _____

Keys to Problem Solving (Part Two)

You have learned that a problem can be any task or assignment or project that you need to complete. **Solving a problem involves five different steps or stages.** You learned that the first three steps in critical problem solving are: (1) define the problem and set a goal for change; (2) brainstorm possible solutions or answers; and (3) evaluate all the possible solutions. You will learn about the remaining two steps in this chapter.

After you have defined your problem, brainstormed possible solutions, and evaluated them, it is time for the fourth step in the critical problem-solving process. **Step four is "Choose a solution and make a plan of action."** Suppose that you and a friend are trying to solve the problem of not having enough time to eat lunch at school. You and your friend have already defined the problem (not having enough time) and set a goal for change (having at least 25 minutes to eat). You have also brainstormed possible solutions (bring lunch from home, don't eat, or get in the lunch line earlier). In Step four you must now choose one of the solutions and write a plan of action of how to carry it out.

The final step in the critical problem solving process is Step five, "Evaluation and Modification." This is the time when you stop and decide whether or not the solution you chose is working. Ask yourself questions such as: "Has the solution solved the problem?" or, "Are there still areas of concern in the situation?" If you can answer "yes" to the first question, and "no" to the second one, the problem-solving process is complete. On the other hand, if you must answer "no" to the first question, and "yes" to the second, you need to make **modifications or changes** in the solution.

Making modifications in the solution will involve going back to Step 3 and reviewing all the possible solutions. You may need to choose a different possible solution. Or you may just need to make some changes in the solution you picked first. After you have done one of these actions, it is time to continue to steps four and five again.

Keys to Problem Solving (Part Two)

1. **Choose one of the problems described below and use the graphic organizer to make a plan for finding a solution.**

Choose one:

a) Jamie has just moved to a new town. School will start in ten days. Jamie doesn't know anyone who will be going to her elementary school. She is beginning to feel like she doesn't even want to go to school any more. What should she do?

b) Basketball try-outs are in two weeks. Stanley has been practicing every night with his dad. Stanley is worried that his friend, Nick, will be chosen for the team and he won't. Stanley's dad tells him that everything will be okay, but he is still worried. What should he do?

c) Trisha has a new baby brother. Now it seems that everyone pays attention to the baby and not to her. Trisha is feeling left out. She's even thinking about running away to her grandma's house. What should she do?

Problem Solving

Describe the Problem

_____

_____

Possible Solutions

1._____

2._____

3._____

Most Logical Solution

_____

_____

Plan to Use the Solution

_____

_____

Evaluation and Modification

_____

_____

Keys to Being a Critical Thinker

1. **Place a check mark (✔) next to each statement that best describes a critical thinker.**

a) ◯ Another student just told Ken that their teacher, Mrs. Griffin, is moving next week. Ken did not say a word to anyone before he went to Mrs. Griffin to find out the facts about her move. Mrs. Griffin tells Ken that she has decided to move to a new house, but she is not going to change jobs.

b) ◯ Beth is confused. Her teacher is explaining how to work a new type of math problem and Beth is having trouble understanding her. When the teacher asks if there are any questions, Beth just sits there and doesn't raise her hand. She is too embarrassed to admit that she doesn't understand.

c) ◯ Julio and Armand love the New York Yankees. They like to tell people that the Yankees have won more games than any other Major League team. One day, Tina and Lori show them the web site, http://www.baseball-reference.com/teams, which says that the San Francisco Giants have won the most games in the Major League. The boys think about this fact and decide that even though they love the Yankees, they won't brag about them being the "winning-est team" of all time again.

d) ◯ Nancy's little sister always asks Nancy's opinion about what she wears. Today Nancy is studying for a big test in social studies and her sister runs into her room. She says, "How do I look?" Nancy tells her she looks just fine without raising her eyes from the book.

e) ◯ Jack's teacher just announced that space scientists have just discovered a new planet in the solar system. Jack just keeps reading his library book because he is not curious about new discoveries in science.

f) ◯ Jenna is trying to persuade her friends to spend the night at her house. The girls are having trouble making up their minds because another friend is having a big skating party that night. Finally, Jenna tells them that her mom will buy them new outfits if they come to her sleep-over. The trouble is that Jenna's mom doesn't have enough money to buy clothes for all the girls.

2. **Place a check mark (✔) next to each quality that a good critical thinker should possess.**

a) ◯ honesty   **b)** ◯ beauty   **c)** ◯ curiosity

d) ◯ dependability   **e)** ◯ quick-tempered   **f)** ◯ fair-mindedness

g) ◯ inattentive   **h)** ◯ disorganized and messy

Keys to Being a Critical Thinker

You have studied many of the things you must *do* to be a critical thinker. Now it is time to talk about some of the **attributes or characteristics that critical thinkers have**:

- A critical thinker is <u>a "question asker."</u>

- A critical thinker <u>is able to admit when he or she does not understand something.</u>

- A critical thinker <u>is curious (eager to know things) about life.</u>

- A critical thinker <u>is interested in finding new solutions.</u>

- A critical thinker <u>listens carefully to others and gives them feedback.</u>

- A critical thinker <u>knows that critical thinking is a lifelong process.</u>

- A critical thinker <u>waits to make a judgment until he or she has considered all the facts.</u>

- A critical thinker <u>looks for evidence to support his or her theories and beliefs.</u>

- A critical thinker <u>looks for proof.</u>

- A critical thinker <u>changes his or her opinions when other facts are found.</u>

- A critical thinker <u>recognizes when information is incorrect or not related to the problem at hand.</u>

There are many benefits or rewards for being a critical thinker. You will find that other students will begin to look to you as a leader. They will want to know what you think about situations and events. Your opinion will become important to them because they have learned that you take the time to consider the facts and then come to a decision. Your friends and classmates will soon learn that you are honest with them and yourself. They will also find that you are not the kind of person who can be manipulated or controlled by the actions of others. All in all, being a critical thinker is a very cool thing to be!

The Reading Watch Dog says,

"Out of the questions of students come most of the world's creative ideas and discoveries."

Keys to Being a Critical Thinker

1. Write a paragraph of at least five sentences describing yourself as a critical thinker. Use the qualities we discussed on the previous page as a guide for thinking.

_____

_____

_____

_____

_____

_____

_____

2. Circle the word True if the statement is true. Circle the word False if it's false.

a) A good critical thinker knows the difference between facts and opinions.

    True   **False**

b) A good critical thinker does not take time to find out whether information is true or not.

    True   **False**

c) A good critical thinker will try to predict the outcome or results of actions or plans.

    True   **False**

d) A good critical thinker is always concerned with finding out the truth.

    True   **False**

e) A good critical thinker does not take the time to give feedback to other people.

    True   **False**

f) A good critical thinker compares the similarities and differences of concepts.

    True   **False**

Keys to Using Critical Thinking Skills to Have Fun

Use your critical thinking skills to solve each of these easy puzzles.

1. **Answer quickly. Starting with an empty barrel, which happens first?**

a) 2/3 full   b) 1/4 empty

c) 1/2 full   d) 3/4 empty

2. **QUESTION: I have many feathers to help me fly. I have a body and head, but I'm not alive. It is your strength which determines how far I go. You can hold me in your hand, but I'm never thrown. What am I?**

3. **This is an unusual paragraph. I'm curious how quickly you can find out what is so unusual about it. It looks so plain you would think nothing is wrong with it. In fact, nothing is wrong with it! It is unusual though. Study it, and think about it, but you still may not find anything odd. But if you work at it a bit, you might find out. Try to do so without any coaching!**

4. **QUESTION: You are walking through a field, and you find something to eat. It doesn't have bones, and it doesn't have meat. You pick it up and put it into your pocket. You take it home and put it on a shelf, but 3 days later it walks away. What is it?**

5. **A man was outside taking a walk when it began to rain. He did not have an umbrella and he wasn't wearing a hat. His clothes were soaked, yet not a single hair on his head got wet. How could this happen?**

Translate these old proverbs (feel free to use your dictionary):

6. "A vessel under optical supervision never reaches the temperature of 212 degrees F (100 degrees C)."

7. "Taciturnity is aurous."

Keys to Using Critical Thinking Skills to Have Fun

You have learned that critical thinking skills are very helpful to you in your school work and daily life. **The more often you think critically, the better your chances are to grow up to be an educated and useful citizen.** However, have you ever thought that using critical thinking skills can be fun? There are many activities and professions that require you to use critical thinking skills. And they are still loads of fun.

Do you like solving mysteries? **Good detectives use critical thinking skills all the time. They look for evidence.** They determine whether the witnesses are telling the truth. They have to be honest. They notice details and give feedback to other people.

Do you like finding out new facts or discovering new places and things? **Scientists, inventors, and archeologists do these kinds of things every day.** If you study one of these subjects in college, you will be able to have fun and earn a good living at the same time.

Do you like solving problems and making people feel better? **Doctors, nurses, physical therapists, and psychologists get to do these things in their work.** Using your critical thinking skills can help you prepare to be the kind of person who helps other people.

There are hundreds and hundreds of other kinds of jobs that require you to use your critical thinking skills. Remember that critical thinking happens when you judge, decide, or solve a problem. The key to using your critical thinking skills is deciding what you want to be and then preparing yourself to be it!

Throughout your life you will find games and activities that require you to think critically and are also fun to do. This chapter will give you some examples of these kinds of activities.

The Reading Watch Dog says,
"It's lots of fun to use your brain to accomplish the impossible."

Keys to Using Critical Thinking Skills to Have Fun

Use your critical thinking skills to answer the following riddles:

1. What do you get when you cross an automobile with a household animal?

_____

2. Where do fish keep their money?

_____

3. What goes around and around the wood but never goes into the wood?

_____

4. I am the beginning of sorrow, and the end of sickness. You cannot express happiness without me, yet I am in the midst of crosses. I am always in risk, yet never in danger. You may find me in the sun, but I am never seen out of darkness.

_____

5 What word looks the same upside down and backwards? (hint: it is something a person or animal does in the water)

_____

6. Follow the instructions carefully, ONE LINE AT A TIME. Be sure to do exactly what it says before moving to the next instruction. You can keep track of your answers by writing them into the spaces provided beside each instruction.

1) Write down the number of the month you were born:	
2) Multiply it by 4:	
3) Add 13:	
4) Multiply the result by 25:	
5) Subtract 200:	
6) Add the day of the month on which you were born:	
7) Multiply by 2:	
8) Subtract 40:	
9) Multiply the result by 50:	
10) Add the last two digits of the year of your birth:	
11) Finally, subtract 10,500:	

Do you notice something odd about your answer? It should be the numbers representing your birth month, date, and the last two numbers of the year you were born!

Critical Thinking CC1118

Sometimes people do things over and over again before they are successful. Dr. Seuss, for example, sent his first book to 27 publishers before it was accepted. Write about how you — or someone you know — succeeded because you or that person kept trying.

_____
_____
_____
_____
_____
_____
_____
_____
_____

📝 Writing Task # 2

Now that you have studied about critical thinking, it is your turn to describe the kind of critical thinker you want to become. Feel free to look back over the chapters and your notes. Be sure to include as many characteristics of a good critical thinker as you can.

_____
_____
_____
_____
_____
_____
_____
_____
_____

Writing Task #3

Everyone loves a mystery and everyone will certainly love yours! Use all of your critical thinking and creative skills to turn the following story prompt into a spine-chilling mystery. Good luck!

The Case of the Holiday Party

The house was quiet the night before our big holiday party. I went to check on the decorations when I saw that all the presents were gone.

_____

_____

_____

_____

_____

_____

Writing Task #4

Now it's time to take yourself and all of your critical thinking and writing skills into a time machine! This time machine can travel forward or backward. Be sure to tell how you got the machine, the time and place to which you traveled, and what happened to you there.

_____

_____

_____

_____

_____

_____

_____

_____

Look carefully at the photo below. Now write a story about how the bike got where it is. What happened? How did it happen? Let your critical thinking skills flow.

- -

📝 Writing Task # 6

Looks may not be everything, but they are important! What would happen if you woke up one day and found that everyone in the world looked the same?

Crossword

Word List
anticipate
attributes
brainstorm
conclusion
consequences
critical
evaluate
facts
independent

Word List
inference
logic
modifications
opinions
problem
reason
solution
thinking
value

Across

2. Expect
6. A state of difficulty that needs to be settled or a question that needs to be answered.
9. A conclusion that you came to in your mind based on something else that you believe to be true.
11. Characteristics
13. Answers
15. Free to make choices
16. Changes
17. The process of using your mind to consider things carefully
18. The effects or results of a decision or action

Down

1. A collection of guiding, positive beliefs or rules that a person follows in life.
3. Measure the quality of something
4. Write down all the answers to a problem that come to mind.
5. Clearly stated information that can be proven
7. The art of reasoning
8. Logical thinking
10. _____ Thinking
12. Drawing a _____
14. Beliefs based on feelings

Word Search

Find the following key words from the story. The words are written horizontally, vertically, diagonally and some are even backwards.

anticipate   creative   fair-minded   modifications   reason
attributes   critical thinking   independent   opinions   solution
brainstorm   evaluate   inference   organized   values
consequences   facts   manipulated   problem

c	r	i	t	i	c	a	l	t	h	i	n	k	i	n	g
o	s	n	f	m	a	n	i	p	u	l	a	t	e	d	u
n	h	d	e	g	h	t	n	a	s	f	h	j	l	i	t
s	t	e	b	r	a	i	n	s	t	o	r	m	n	f	n
e	o	p	a	s	v	c	m	b	k	h	e	h	o	a	d
q	d	e	f	n	o	i	t	u	l	o	s	e	s	o	l
u	e	n	k	l	o	p	e	w	h	k	j	y	a	d	k
e	z	d	d	s	f	a	i	r	m	i	n	d	e	d	s
n	i	e	r	t	o	t	n	k	o	y	r	a	r	f	n
c	n	n	b	g	a	e	f	w	d	h	q	u	i	b	m
e	a	t	s	v	h	m	e	i	i	h	w	f	b	m	s
s	g	y	o	k	g	r	r	v	f	d	f	g	a	e	e
x	r	d	i	v	u	b	e	a	i	g	m	y	u	a	t
u	o	p	i	n	i	o	n	s	c	t	u	l	s	d	u
j	n	b	r	x	a	h	c	g	a	r	a	h	t	r	b
s	f	j	n	o	h	a	e	s	t	v	d	e	b	c	i
r	g	u	r	l	b	p	n	q	i	f	b	c	r	k	r
q	w	e	t	h	j	l	n	b	o	a	s	n	b	c	t
e	t	a	u	l	a	v	e	h	n	s	e	y	i	u	t
l	m	h	d	b	n	o	p	m	s	t	c	a	f	o	a

     Critical Thinking CC1118

Comprehension Quiz

Put a "T" in front of each true statement and put an "F" in front of each false statement.

☐ **1.** Critical thinking is what happens when you judge, decide, or solve a problem.

☐ **2.** Values are not important to a good critical thinker.

☐ **3.** Learning to think for yourself is important to being successful in life.

☐ **4.** Most critical thinkers do not like to explore new ideas.

☐ **5.** Reason is logical thinking.

☐ **6.** Critical thinkers are dependent thinkers.

☐ **7.** A good independent critical thinker is also a good listener.

☐ **8.** Honesty is not very important to good critical thinkers.

☐ **9.** An independent thinker knows it's better to make mistakes than to accept someone else's opinions about everything in life.

☐ **10.** Organized means "orderly and effective."

10

Write the answers to the following questions.

11. What is an inference?

1

_____

12. What is the difference between a fact and an opinion? Give an example of a fact and an example of an opinion.

4

_____

13. What does the following statement mean? "A good critical thinker anticipates consequences."

2

_____

14. What are three organization tips that good critical thinkers can use?

3

_____

SUBTOTAL: **/20**

After You Read

Comprehension Quiz

Put an "F" in front of each FACT and put an "O" in front of each OPINION.

15. ☐ People need to eat food in order to survive.

16. ☐ The best foods to eat are green beans and corn on the cob.

17. ☐ We saw the most exciting adventure movie in the world last night!

18. ☐ The movie received excellent reviews from the critics.

19. ☐ Everyone needs to read a good mystery book about once a month.

5

Circle the cause and underline the effect in each statement below.

20. It was raining so I brought my red umbrella with me.

21. Because the truck was out of gas it would not start when Tim tried the ignition.

22. I get good grades in English because it is my favorite subject.

23. Marie is a great pianist because she practices three hours a day!

24. I had to reboot my computer because the screen froze.

5

Complete the following graphic organizer by filling in the five parts of the critical problem-solving process.

THE CRITICAL PROBLEM-SOLVING PROCESS

25. The five steps in the critical problem solving process are:

1: _____

2: _____

3: _____

4: _____

5

5: _____

SUBTOTAL: **/15**

1.

Answers may vary. Accept any reasonable response.

2.

Answers may vary. Accept any reasonable response.

15

1.

i) ✓ A

ii) ✓ A

iii) ✓ A

iv) ✓ A

v) ✓ A

vi) ✓ A

13

1.

Answers may vary. Accept any reasonable responses.

12

1.

A — 3
B — 4
C — 5
D — 2
E — 1

2.

a, c, e, g, i, and j should be checked.

10

1.

a) creative and critical thinking

b) Thinking

c) Creative

d) Critical

2.

a) Involves critical thinking

b) Involves critical thinking

c) Does not involve critical thinking

d) Involves critical thinking

e) Does not involve critical thinking

f) Involves critical thinking

g) Does not involve critical thinking

h) Involves critical thinking

9

1.

a) False

b) True

c) False

d) True

2.

i) ✓ B

ii) ✓ A

iii) ✓ A

iv) ✓ B

7

1.

15 - Useless without the relevant tables and a chronometer.

1 - Critical for signaling.

14 - There are NO mosquitoes in the middle of the Atlantic Ocean.

3 - Vital to restore fluids lost through perspiration.

4 - This is your basic food intake.

13 - Worthless without navigation equipment.

9 - Useful as a life preserver if someone fell overboard.

2 - Critical for signaling. The mixture will float on water and could be ignited using the matches.

12 - You would be out of range of any radio station.

5 - Can be used to collect rain water and shelter from the wind and waves.

10 - To repel sharks.

11 - Contains 80% alcohol, which means it can be used as an antiseptic for any injuries. It would cause dehydration if drunk.

8 - Could be used to lash people or equipment together to prevent being washed overboard.

6 - Your reserve food supply.

7 - Ranked lower than the chocolate as there is no guarantee you will catch any fish.

24

1.

a) ii)

b) iii)

c) i)

d) ii)

e) i)

2.

Answers may vary. Accept any reasonable response.

22

1.

i) ✓ B

ii) ✓ A

iii) ✓ C

iv) ✓ D

v) ✓ B

Explanations may vary. Accept any reasonable response.

21

1.

a) True

b) False

c) True

d) False

e) False

2.

a) F

b) ○

c) ○

d) F

e) F

19

1.

Answers may vary. Accept any reasonable response.

18

1.

a, c, e, g, and j should be checked.

2.

Answers may vary. Accept any reasonable response.

16

1. Answers may vary. Accept any reasonable response.

2. Answers may vary. Accept any reasonable response.

(33)

1.

a) Problems are "states of difficulty that need to be settled or questions that need to be answered." Problem solving is finding the answers to the problems.

b) Answers may vary. Accept any reasonable response.

c) The man.

d) Mt. Everest — it just had not been discovered yet.

e) Jimmy, of course!

2.

a) True

b) False

c) False

d) True

(31)

1. Answers may vary. Accept any reasonable response.

(30)

1.

A 4

B 2

C 6

D 3

E 1

F 5

2.

a) 3

b) 1

c) 4

d) 2

(28)

1. Answers may vary. Accept any reasonable response.

2. Answers may vary. Accept any reasonable response.

(27)

1.

a) O

b) F

c) F

d) O

e) O

f) O

g) O

h) O

i) F

j) O

2.

a) True

b) False

c) False

d) False

e) True

(25)

1. A car-pet

2. In a river-bank

3. Tree bark

4. The letter 's'

5. SWIMS

6. The answer should be the student's month, day, and last two numbers of his or her birth year.

1. d) ¾ empty: since ¾ empty means ¼ full.

2. An arrow.

3. The letter 'e', which is the most common letter in the English language, does not appear once in the paragraph.

4. An egg.

5. He was bald.

6. "A watched pot never boils."

7. "Silence is golden."

1. Answers may vary. Accept any reasonable response.

2.
a) True
b) False
c) True
d) True
e) False
f) True

1. a) and c).

2. a), c), d), and f).

1. Answers may vary. Accept any reasonable response.

1.
a) Any task or assignment or project that you need to complete.

b) Define the problem and set a goal for change; brainstorm possible solutions or answers; and evaluate all the possible solutions.

2.
a) A pizza was in the box. Sandy must be right because no one else said pizza.

b) The dog is white, has short hair, wears a blue collar, and has a short tail.

To arrive at the answer, make a chart to display the children's descriptions.

Word Search Answers

Across

2. anticipate
6. problem
9. inference
11. attributes
13. solution
15. independent
16. modifications
17. thinking
18. consequences

Down

1. value
3. evaluate
4. brainstorm
5. facts
7. logic
8. reason
10. critical
12. conclusion
14. opinions

---

1. T
2. F
3. T
4. F
5. T
6. F
7. T
8. F
9. T
10. T

11. Inference is a conclusion you come to in your mind based on something else that you believe to be true.

12. A fact can be proven. An opinion is based on beliefs and feelings and cannot be proven. Fact – This book is about critical thinking skills. Opinion – This is the best book about critical thinking skills I've ever read!

13. A good critical thinker thinks about the results of a plan or action before he begins the plan or action.

14. Answers may vary. Accept any reasonable response.

EZ✓

15. F
16. O
17. O
18. F
19. O

20-24.
- It was raining / I brought my red umbrella
- The truck was out of gas / it would not start
- I get good grades / it is my favorite subject.
- Marie is a great pianist / she practices three hours a day!
- had to reboot / the screen froze

25.
1: Define the problem and set a goal for change;
2: brainstorm possible solutions or answers;
3: evaluate all the possible solutions;
4: choose a solution and make a plan of action;
5: evaluation and modification.

Critical Thinkers

Critical thinkers are:

- curious about the world.

- creative questioners.

- frequently asking "why?" and seeking reasons to defend a position.

- interested only in credible sources of information.

- able to take into account the total situation or context when interpreting something.

- relevant thinkers who stick to the main point.

- always looking for alternative explanations, positions, or arguments.

- open-minded and who seriously consider points of view other than their own.

- willing to change a position when the evidence is sufficient to make them do so.

- able to withhold judgment when the evidence is insufficient.

- eager to seek precision.

- able to realize the limits of knowing; hence they look for probability rather than proof.

- able to realize the role of personal bias in the process of knowing something.

- able to deal in an orderly manner with the parts of a complex whole and anticipate the next step in a process.

- sensitive to the feelings, levels of knowledge, and degree of sophistication of others when presenting their findings.

- able to apply critical thinking abilities to a wide variety of subjects.

Making Decisions

Title/Topic: _____

My Problems ➡️

I Think That ➡️

I'll Find Out By ➡️

I Found That ➡️

Conclusions ➡️

Class Decision Chart

Decision to be made:

Qualities

Possible Solutions

Score

1.					
2.					
3.					
4.					
5.					
6.					
7.					
8.					

Final decision:

Prediction With Evidence

Name: _____ Date: _____

I predict that:

Evidence #1

Source:

Evidence #2

Source:

Evidence #3

Source:

Evidence #4

Source:

Evidence #5

Source:

Who, What, When, Where, Why & How

Who

What

When

Where

Why

How

Text & Subtext: Drawing Inferences

● ● ● ● ● ● ● ● ● ● ● ● ● ● ● ● ● ● ●

Name: _____ **Date:** _____

Title/Topic: _____

What the text says, in your own words

Quotation

What the subtext is

What the text says, in your own words

Quotation

What the subtext is

- **RSIT.5.1** Quote accurately from a text when explaining what the text says explicitly and when drawing inferences from the text.
- **RSIT.5.2** Determine two or more main ideas of a text and explain how they are supported by key details; summarize the text.
- **RSIT.5.4** Determine the meaning of general academic and domain-specific words and phrases in a text relevant to a grade 5 topics or subject area.
- **RSIT.5.5** Compare and contrast the overall structure of events, ideas, concepts, or information in two or more texts.
- **RSIT.5.7** Draw on information from multiple print or digital sources, demonstrating the ability to locate an answer to a question quickly or to solve a problem efficiently.
- **RSIT.5.8** Explain how an author uses reasons and evidence to support particular points in a text, identifying which reasons and evidence support which point(s).
- **RSIT.5.9** Integrate information from several texts on the same topic in order to write or speak about the subject knowledgeably.
- **RSIT.6.1** Cite textual evidence to support analysis of what the text says explicitly as well as inferences drawn from the text.
- **RSIT.6.2** Determine a central idea of a text and how it is conveyed through particular details; provide a summary of the text distinct from personal opinions or judgments.
- **RSIT.6.4** Determine the meaning of words and phrases as they are used in a text, including figurative, connotative, and technical meanings.
- **RSIT.6.5** Analyze how a particular sentence, paragraph, chapter, or section fits into the overall structure of a text and contributes to the development of the ideas.
- **RSIT.6.8** Trace and evaluate the argument and specific claims in a text, distinguishing claims that are supported by reasons and evidence from claims that are not.
- **RSIT.7.1** Cite several pieces of textual evidence to support analysis of what the text says explicitly as well as inferences drawn from the text.
- **RSIT.7.2** Determine two or more central ideas in a text and analyze their development over the course of the text; provide an objective summary of the text.
- **RSIT.7.4** Determine the meaning of words and phrases as they are used in a text, including figurative, connotative, and technical meanings; analyze the impact of a specific word choice on meaning and tone.
- **RSIT.7.5** Analyze the structure an author uses to organize a text, including how the major sections contribute to the whole and to the development of the ideas.
- **RSIT.7.8** Trace and evaluate the argument and specific claims in a text, assessing whether the reasoning is sound and the evidence is relevant and sufficient to support the claims.
- **RSIT.8.1** Cite the textual evidence that most strongly supports an analysis of what the text says explicitly as well as inferences drawn from the text.
- **RSIT.8.2** Determine a central idea of a text and analyze its development over the course of the text, including its relationship to supporting ideas; provide an objective summary of the text.
- **RSIT.8.4** Determine the meaning of words and phrases as they are used in a text, including figurative, connotative, and technical meanings; analyze the impact of specific word choices on meaning and tone, including analogies or allusions to other texts.
- **RSIT.8.5** Analyze in detail the structure of a specific paragraph in a text, including the role of particular sentences in developing and refining a key concept.
- **RSIT.8.8** Delineate and evaluate the argument and specific claims in a text, assessing whether the reasoning is sound and the evidence is relevant and sufficient; recognize when irrelevant evidence is introduced.
- **RSFS.5.4** Read with sufficient accuracy and fluency to support comprehension.
- **WS.5.4** Produce clear and coherent writing in which the development and organization are appropriate to task, purpose, and audience.
- **WS.5.7** Conduct short research projects that use several sources to build knowledge through investigation of different aspects of a topic.
- **WS.5.8** Recall relevant information from experiences or gather relevant information from print and digital sources; summarize or paraphrase information in notes and finished work, and provide a list of sources.
- **WS.5.9** Draw evidence from literary or informational texts to support analysis, reflection, and research.
- **WS.5.10** Write routinely over extended time frames and shorter time frames for a range of discipline-specific tasks, purposes, and audiences.
- **WS.6.1** Write arguments to support claims with clear reasons and relevant evidence.
- **WS.6.2** Write informative/explanatory texts to examine a topic and convey ideas, concepts, and information through the selection, organization, and analysis of relevant content.
- **WS.6.3** Write narratives to develop real or imagined experiences or events using effective technique, relevant descriptive details, and well-structured event sequences.
- **WS.6.4** Produce clear and coherent writing in which the development, organization, and style are appropriate to task, purpose, and audience.
- **WS.6.7** Conduct short research projects to answer a question, drawing on several sources and refocusing the inquiry when appropriate.
- **WS.6.8** Gather relevant information from multiple print and digital sources; assess the credibility of each source; and quote or paraphrase the data and conclusions of others while avoiding plagiarism and providing basic bibliographic information for sources.
- **WS.6.9** Draw evidence from literary or informational texts to support analysis, reflection, and research.
- **WS.6.10** Write routinely over extended time frames and shorter time frames for a range of discipline-specific tasks, purposes, and audiences.
- **WS.7.1** Write arguments to support claims with clear reasons and relevant evidence.
- **WS.7.2** Write informative/explanatory texts to examine a topic and convey ideas, concepts, and information through the selection, organization, and analysis of relevant content.
- **WS.7.3** Write narratives to develop real or imagined experiences or events using effective technique, relevant descriptive details, and well-structured event sequences.
- **WS.7.4** Produce clear and coherent writing in which the development, organization, and style are appropriate to task, purpose, and audience.
- **WS.7.7** Conduct short research projects to answer a question, drawing on several sources and generating additional related, focused questions for further research and investigation.
- **WS.7.8** Gather relevant information from multiple print and digital sources, using search terms effectively; assess the credibility and accuracy of each source; and quote or paraphrase the data and conclusions of others while avoiding plagiarism and following a standard format for citation.
- **WS.7.9** Draw evidence from literary or informational texts to support analysis, reflection, and research.
- **WS.7.10** Write routinely over extended time frames and shorter time frames for a range of discipline-specific tasks, purposes, and audiences.
- **WS.8.1** Write arguments to support claims with clear reasons and relevant evidence.
- **WS.8.2** Write informative/explanatory texts to examine a topic and convey ideas, concepts, and information through the selection, organization, and analysis of relevant content.
- **WS.8.3** Write narratives to develop real or imagined experiences or events using effective technique, relevant descriptive details, and well-structured event sequences.
- **WS.8.4** Produce clear and coherent writing in which the development, organization, and style are appropriate to task, purpose, and audience.

- **WS.8.7** Conduct short research projects to answer a question, drawing on several sources and generating additional related, focused questions that allow for multiple avenues of exploration.
- **WS.8.8** Gather relevant information from multiple print and digital sources, using search terms effectively; assess the credibility and accuracy of each source; and quote or paraphrase the data and conclusions of others while avoiding plagiarism and following a standard format for citation.
- **WS.8.9** Draw evidence from literary or informational texts to support analysis, reflection, and research.
- **WS.8.10** Write routinely over extended time frames and shorter time frames for a range of discipline-specific tasks, purposes, and audiences.
- **SLS.5.1** Engage effectively in a range of collaborative discussions with diverse partners on grade 5 topics and texts, building on others' ideas and expressing their own clearly.
- **SLS.5.2** Summarize a written text read aloud or information presented in diverse media and formats, including visually, quantitatively, and orally.
- **SLS.5.3** Summarize the points a speaker makes and explain how each claim is supported by reasons and evidence.
- **SLS.5.6** Adapt speech to a variety of contexts and tasks, using formal English when appropriate to task and situation.
- **SLS.6.1** Engage effectively in a range of collaborative discussions with diverse partners on grade 6 topics, texts, and issues, building on others' ideas and expressing their own clearly.
- **SLS.6.4** Present claims and findings, sequencing ideas logically and using pertinent descriptions, facts, and details to accentuate main ideas or themes; use appropriate eye contact, adequate volume, and clear pronunciation.
- **SLS.6.6** Adapt speech to a variety of contexts and tasks, demonstrating command of formal English when indicated or appropriate.
- **SLS.7.1** Engage effectively in a range of collaborative discussions with diverse partners on grade 7 topics, texts, and issues, building on others' ideas and expressing their own clearly.
- **SLS.7.4** Present claims and findings, emphasizing salient points in a focused, coherent manner with relevant evidence, sound valid reasoning, and well-chosen details; use appropriate eye contact, adequate volume, and clear pronunciation.
- **SLS.7.6** Adapt speech to a variety of contexts and tasks, demonstrating command of formal English when indicated or appropriate.
- **SLS.8.1** Engage effectively in a range of collaborative discussions with diverse partners on grade 8 topics, texts, and issues, building on others' ideas and expressing their own clearly.
- **SLS.8.2** Analyze the purpose of information presented in diverse media and formats and evaluate the motives behind its presentation.
- **SLS.8.4** Present claims and findings, emphasizing salient points in a focused, coherent manner with relevant evidence, sound valid reasoning, and well-chosen details; use appropriate eye contact, adequate volume, and clear pronunciation.
- **SLS.8.6** Adapt speech to a variety of contexts and tasks, demonstrating command of formal English when indicated or appropriate.
- **LS.5.3** Use knowledge of language and its conventions when writing, speaking, reading, or listening.
- **LS.5.4** Determine or clarify the meaning of unknown and multiple-meaning words and phrases based on grade 5 reading and content, choosing flexibly from a range of strategies.
- **LS.5.5** Demonstrate understanding of figurative language, word relationships, and nuances in word meanings.
- **LS.5.6** Acquire and use accurately grade-appropriate general academic and domain-specific words and phrases, including those that signal contrast, addition, and other logical relationships.
- **LS.6.3** Use knowledge of language and its conventions when writing, speaking, reading, or listening.
- **LS.6.4** Determine or clarify the meaning of unknown and multiple-meaning words and phrases based on *grade 6 reading and content*, choosing flexibly from a range of strategies.
- **LS.6.5** Demonstrate understanding of figurative language, word relationships, and nuances in word meanings.
- **LS.7.3** Use knowledge of language and its conventions when writing, speaking, reading, or listening.
- **LS.7.4** Determine or clarify the meaning of unknown and multiple-meaning words and phrases based on *grade 7 reading and content*, choosing flexibly from a range of strategies
- **LS.7.5** Demonstrate understanding of figurative language, word relationships, and nuances in word meanings
- **LS.8.3** Use knowledge of language and its conventions when writing, speaking, reading, or listening.
- **LS.8.4** Determine or clarify the meaning of unknown and multiple-meaning words or phrases based on *grade 8 reading and content*, choosing flexibly from a range of strategies.
- **LS.8.5** Demonstrate understanding of figurative language, word relationships, and nuances in word meanings.
- **LS.8.6** Acquire and use accurately grade-appropriate general academic and domain-specific words and phrases; gather vocabulary knowledge when considering a word or phrase important to comprehension or expression.

Publication Listing

Ask Your Dealer About Our Complete Line

SOCIAL STUDIES - Software

ITEM #	TITLE
	MAPPING SKILLS SERIES
CC7770	Grades PK-2 Mapping Skills with Google Earth
CC7771	Grades 3-5 Mapping Skills with Google Earth
CC7772	Grades 6-8 Mapping Skills with Google Earth
CC7773	Grades PK-8 Mapping Skills with Google Earth Big Box

SOCIAL STUDIES - Books

ITEM #	TITLE
	MAPPING SKILLS SERIES
CC5786	Grades PK-2 Mapping Skills with Google Earth
CC5787	Grades 3-5 Mapping Skills with Google Earth
CC5788	Grades 6-8 Mapping Skills with Google Earth
CC5789	Grades PK-8 Mapping Skills with Google Earth Big Book
	NORTH AMERICAN GOVERNMENTS SERIES
CC5757	American Government
CC5758	Canadian Government
CC5759	Mexican Government
CC5760	Governments of North America Big Book
	WORLD GOVERNMENTS SERIES
CC5761	World Political Leaders
CC5762	World Electoral Processes
CC5763	Capitalism vs. Communism
CC5777	World Politics Big Book
	WORLD CONFLICT SERIES
CC5511	American Revolutionary War
CC5500	American Civil War
CC5512	American Wars Big Book
CC5501	World War I
CC5502	World War II
CC5503	World Wars I & II Big Book
CC5505	Korean War
CC5506	Vietnam War
CC5507	Korean & Vietnam Wars Big Book
CC5508	Persian Gulf War (1990-1991)
CC5509	Iraq War (2003-2010)
CC5510	Gulf Wars Big Book
	WORLD CONTINENTS SERIES
CC5750	North America
CC5751	South America
CC5768	The Americas Big Book
CC5752	Europe
CC5753	Africa
CC5754	Asia
CC5755	Australia
CC5756	Antarctica
	WORLD CONNECTIONS SERIES
CC5782	Culture, Society & Globalization
CC5783	Economy & Globalization
CC5784	Technology & Globalization
CC5785	Globalization Big Book

REGULAR & REMEDIAL EDUCATION

Reading Level 3-4 Grades 5-8

ENVIRONMENTAL STUDIES - Software

ITEM #	TITLE
	CLIMATE CHANGE SERIES
CC7747	Global Warming: Causes Grades 3-8
CC7748	Global Warming: Effects Grades 3-8
CC7749	Global Warming: Reduction Grades 3-8
CC7750	Global Warming Big Box Grades 3-8

ENVIRONMENTAL STUDIES - Books

ITEM #	TITLE
	MANAGING OUR WASTE SERIES
CC5764	Waste: At the Source
CC5765	Prevention, Recycling & Conservation
CC5766	Waste: The Global View
CC5767	Waste Management Big Book
	CLIMATE CHANGE SERIES
CC5769	Global Warming: Causes
CC5770	Global Warming: Effects
CC5771	Global Warming: Reduction
CC5772	Global Warming Big Book
	GLOBAL WATER SERIES
CC5773	Conservation: Fresh Water Resources
CC5774	Conservation: Ocean Water Resources
CC5775	Conservation: Waterway Habitats Resources
CC5776	Water Conservation Big Book
	CARBON FOOTPRINT SERIES
CC5778	Reducing Your Own Carbon Footprint
CC5779	Reducing Your School's Carbon Footprint
CC5780	Reducing Your Community's Carbon Footprint
CC5781	Carbon Footprint Big Book

SCIENCE - Software

ITEM #	TITLE
	SPACE AND BEYOND SERIES
CC7557	Solar System Grades 5-8
CC7558	Galaxies & the Universe Grades 5-8
CC7559	Space Travel & Technology Grades 5-8
CC7560	Space Big Box Grades 5-8
	HUMAN BODY SERIES
CC7549	Cells, Skeletal & Muscular Systems Grades 5-8
CC7550	Senses, Nervous & Respiratory Systems Grades 5-8
CC7551	Circulatory, Digestive & Reproductive Systems Grades 5-8
CC7552	Human Body Big Box Grades 5-8
	FORCE, MOTION & SIMPLE MACHINES SERIES
CC7553	Force Grades 3-8
CC7554	Motion Grades 3-8
CC7555	Simple Machines Grades 3-8
CC7556	Force, Motion & Simple Machines Big Box Grades 3-8

SCIENCE - Books

ITEM #	TITLE
	ECOLOGY & THE ENVIRONMENT SERIES
CC4500	Ecosystems
CC4501	Classification & Adaptation
CC4502	Cells
CC4503	Ecology & The Environment Big Book
	MATTER & ENERGY SERIES
CC4504	Properties of Matter
CC4505	Atoms, Molecules & Elements
CC4506	Energy
CC4507	The Nature of Matter Big Book
	FORCE & MOTION SERIES
CC4508	Force
CC4509	Motion
CC4510	Simple Machines
CC4511	Force, Motion & Simple Machines Big Book
	SPACE & BEYOND SERIES
CC4512	Solar System
CC4513	Galaxies & The Universe
CC4514	Travel & Technology
CC4515	Space Big Book
	HUMAN BODY SERIES
CC4516	Cells, Skeletal & Muscular Systems
CC4517	Nervous, Senses & Respiratory Systems
CC4518	Circulatory, Digestive & Reproductive Systems
CC4519	Human Body Big Book

VISIT:

www.CLASSROOM COMPLETE PRESS.com

To view sample pages from each book

14-1

LITERATURE KITS™- Books

ITEM #	TITLE
	GRADES 1-2
CC2100	Curious George (H. A. Rey)
CC2101	Paper Bag Princess (Robert N. Munsch)
CC2102	Stone Soup (Marcia Brown)
CC2103	The Very Hungry Caterpillar (Eric Carle)
CC2104	Where the Wild Things Are (Maurice Sendak)
	GRADES 3-4
CC2300	Babe: The Gallant Pig (Dick King-Smith)
CC2301	Because of Winn-Dixie (Kate DiCamillo)
CC2302	The Tale of Despereaux (Kate DiCamillo)
CC2303	James and the Giant Peach (Roald Dahl)
CC2304	Ramona Quimby, Age 8 (Beverly Cleary)
CC2305	The Mouse and the Motorcycle (Beverly Cleary)
CC2306	Charlotte's Web (E.B. White)
CC2307	Owls in the Family (Farley Mowat)
CC2308	Sarah, Plain and Tall (Patricia MacLachlan)
CC2309	Matilda (Roald Dahl)
CC2310	Charlie & The Chocolate Factory (Roald Dahl)
CC2311	Frindle (Andrew Clements)
CC2312	M.C. Higgins, the Great (Virginia Hamilton)
CC2313	The Family Under The Bridge (N.S. Carlson)
CC2314	The Hundred Penny Box (Sharon Mathis)
CC2315	Cricket in Times Square (George Selden)
	GRADES 5-6
CC2500	Black Beauty (Anna Sewell)
CC2501	Bridge to Terabithia (Katherine Paterson)
CC2502	Bud, Not Buddy (Christopher Paul Curtis)
CC2503	The Egypt Game (Zilpha Keatley Snyder)
CC2504	The Great Gilly Hopkins (Katherine Paterson)
CC2505	Holes (Louis Sachar)
CC2506	Number the Stars (Lois Lowry)
CC2507	The Sign of the Beaver (E.G. Speare)
CC2508	The Whipping Boy (Sid Fleischman)
CC2509	Island of the Blue Dolphins (Scott O'Dell)
CC2510	Underground to Canada (Barbara Smucker)
CC2511	Loser (Jerry Spinelli)
CC2512	The Higher Power of Lucky (Susan Patron)
CC2513	Kira-Kira (Cynthia Kadohata)
CC2514	Dear Mr. Henshaw (Beverly Cleary)
CC2515	The Summer of the Swans (Betsy Byars)
CC2516	Shiloh (Phyllis Reynolds Naylor)
CC2517	A Single Shard (Linda Sue Park)
CC2518	Hoot (Carl Hiaasen)
CC2519	Hatchet (Gary Paulsen)
CC2520	The Giver (Lois Lowry)
CC2521	The Graveyard Book (Neil Gaiman)
CC2522	The View From Saturday (E.L Konigsburg)
CC2523	Hattie Big Sky (Kirby Larson)
CC2524	When You Reach Me (Rebecca Stead)
CC2525	Criss Cross (Lynne Rae Perkins)
CC2526	A Year Down Yonder (Richard Peak)
	GRADES 7-8
CC2700	Cheaper by the Dozen (Frank B. Gilbreth)
CC2701	The Miracle Worker (William Gibson)
CC2702	The Red Pony (John Steinbeck)
CC2703	Treasure Island (Robert Louis Stevenson)
CC2704	Romeo & Juliet (William Shakespeare)
CC2705	Crispin: The Cross of Lead (Avi)

LITERATURE KITS™- Books

ITEM #	TITLE
	GRADES 9-12
CC2001	To Kill A Mockingbird (Harper Lee)
CC2002	Angela's Ashes (Frank McCourt)
CC2003	The Grapes of Wrath (John Steinbeck)
CC2004	The Good Earth (Pearl S. Buck)
CC2005	The Road (Cormac McCarthy)
CC2006	The Old Man and the Sea (Ernest Hemingway)
CC2007	Lord of the Flies (William Golding)
CC2008	The Color Purple (Alice Walker)
CC2009	The Outsiders (S.E. Hinton)
CC2010	Hamlet (William Shakespeare)

LANGUAGE ARTS - Software

ITEM #	TITLE
	WORD FAMILIES SERIES
CC7112	Word Families - Short Vowels Grades PK-2
CC7113	Word Families - Long Vowels Grades PK-2
CC7114	Word Families - Vowels Big Box Grades PK-2
	SIGHT & PICTURE WORDS SERIES
CC7100	High Frequency Sight Words Grades PK-2
CC7101	High Frequency Picture Words Grades PK-2
CC7102	Sight & Picture Words Big Box Grades PK-2
	WRITING SKILLS SERIES
CC7104	How to Write a Paragraph Grades 5-8
CC7105	How to Write a Book Report Grades 5-8
CC7106	How to Write an Essay Grades 5-8
CC7107	Master Writing Big Box Grades 5-8
	READING SKILLS SERIES
CC7108	Reading Comprehension Grades 3-8
CC7109	Literary Devices Grades 3-8
CC7110	Critical Thinking Grades 3-8
CC7111	Master Reading Big Box Grades 3-8

LANGUAGE ARTS - Books

ITEM #	TITLE
	WORD FAMILIES SERIES
CC1110	Word Families - Short Vowels Grades PK-1
CC1111	Word Families - Long Vowels Grades PK-1
CC1112	Word Families - Vowels Big Book Grades K-1
	SIGHT & PICTURE WORDS SERIES
CC1113	High Frequency Sight Words Grades PK-1
CC1114	High Frequency Picture Words Grades PK-1
CC1115	Sight & Picture Words Big Book Grades PK-1
	WRITING SKILLS SERIES
CC1100	How to Write a Paragraph Grades 5-8
CC1101	How to Write a Book Report Grades 5-8
CC1102	How to Write an Essay Grades 5-8
CC1103	Master Writing Big Book Grades 5-8
	READING SKILLS SERIES
CC7108	Reading Comprehension Grades 5-8
CC7109	Literary Devices Grades 5-8
CC7110	Critical Thinking Grades 5-8
CC7111	Master Reading Big Book Grades 5-8
	READING RESPONSE FORMS SERIES
CC1106	Reading Response Forms: Grades 1-2
CC1107	Reading Response Forms: Grades 3-4
CC1108	Reading Response Forms: Grades 5-6
CC1109	Reading Response Forms Big Book: Grades 1-6

MATHEMATICS - Software

ITEM #	TITLE
	PRINCIPLES & STANDARDS OF MATH SERIES
CC7315	Grades PK-2 Five Strands of Math Big Box
CC7316	Grades 3-5 Five Strands of Math Big Box
CC7317	Grades 6-8 Five Strands of Math Big Box

MATHEMATICS - Books

ITEM #	TITLE
	PRINCIPLES & STANDARDS OF MATH SERIES
CC3100	Grades PK-2 Number & Operations Task Sheets
CC3101	Grades PK-2 Algebra Task Sheets
CC3102	Grades PK-2 Geometry Task Sheets
CC3103	Grades PK-2 Measurement Task Sheets
CC3104	Grades PK-2 Data Analysis & Probability Task Sheets
CC3105	Grades PK-2 Five Strands of Math Big Book Task Sheets
CC3106	Grades 3-5 Number & Operations Task Sheets
CC3107	Grades 3-5 Algebra Task Sheets
CC3108	Grades 3-5 Geometry Task Sheets
CC3109	Grades 3-5 Measurement Task Sheets
CC3110	Grades 3-5 Data Analysis & Probability Task Sheets
CC3111	Grades 3-5 Five Strands of Math Big Book Task Sheets
CC3112	Grades 6-8 Number & Operations Task Sheets
CC3113	Grades 6-8 Algebra Task Sheets
CC3114	Grades 6-8 Geometry Task Sheets
CC3115	Grades 6-8 Measurement Task Sheets
CC3116	Grades 6-8 Data Analysis & Probability Task Sheets
CC3117	Grades 6-8 Five Strands of Math Big Book Task Sheets
	PRINCIPLES & STANDARDS OF MATH SERIES
CC3200	Grades PK-2 Number & Operations Drill Sheets
CC3201	Grades PK-2 Algebra Drill Sheets
CC3202	Grades PK-2 Geometry Drill Sheets
CC3203	Grades PK-2 Measurement Drill Sheets
CC3204	Grades PK-2 Data Analysis & Probability Drill Sheets
CC3205	Grades PK-2 Five Strands of Math Big Book Drill Sheets
CC3206	Grades 3-5 Number & Operations Drill Sheets
CC3207	Grades 3-5 Algebra Drill Sheets
CC3208	Grades 3-5 Geometry Drill Sheets
CC3209	Grades 3-5 Measurement Drill Sheets
CC3210	Grades 3-5 Data Analysis & Probability Drill Sheets
CC3211	Grades 3-5 Five Strands of Math Big Book Drill Sheets
CC3212	Grades 6-8 Number & Operations Drill Sheets
CC3213	Grades 6-8 Algebra Drill Sheets
CC3214	Grades 6-8 Geometry Drill Sheets
CC3215	Grades 6-8 Measurement Drill Sheets
CC3216	Grades 6-8 Data Analysis & Probability Drill Sheets
CC3217	Grades 6-8 Five Strands of Math Big Book Drill Sheets
	PRINCIPLES & STANDARDS OF MATH SERIES
CC3300	Grades PK-2 Number & Operations Task & Drill Sheets
CC3301	Grades PK-2 Algebra Task & Drill Sheets
CC3302	Grades PK-2 Geometry Task & Drill Sheets
CC3303	Grades PK-2 Measurement Task & Drill Sheets
CC3304	Grades PK-2 Data Analysis & Probability Task & Drills
CC3306	Grades 3-5 Number & Operations Task & Drill Sheets
CC3307	Grades 3-5 Algebra Task & Drill Sheets
CC3308	Grades 3-5 Geometry Task & Drill Sheets
CC3309	Grades 3-5 Measurement Task & Drill Sheets
CC3310	Grades 3-5 Data Analysis & Probability Task & Drills
CC3312	Grades 6-8 Number & Operations Task & Drill Sheets
CC3313	Grades 6-8 Algebra Task & Drill Sheets
CC3314	Grades 6-8 Geometry Task & Drill Sheets
CC3315	Grades 6-8 Measurement Task & Drill Sheets
CC3316	Grades 6-8 Data Analysis & Probability Task & Drills